THEY CALL ME THE REFUND MAN

HOW YOU CAN START A SUCCESSFUL TAX BUSINESS

NATHANIEL R. MCDANIEL

CONTENTS

INTRODUCTION

The world of taxes can be extremely overwhelming for most people. The number of laws to keep in mind, the deductions that one *might* be able to get, and figuring out the nooks and crannies can all be too complex for most. And yet, for me, an interest in this world and understanding the details has always come naturally. Now it has become my passion.

In fact, I've always prepared my own tax return since I received my first W-2 from my first job. I was working as a bagger at a local grocery store right after high school. Back then, there were no tax software programs or even Internet service. We had to do our taxes all on our own so it turned out to be a good experience for me to learn how to do it completely from scratch.

Income taxes were done by entering information on a paper 1040 US Individual Income Tax Return form. The post office stocked all the 1040 tax forms and the 1040 instruction booklet, which was thick and intimidating. For the typical person, the entire process was intimidating.

For me, however, it felt more like a game. I was curious and wanted to know how the process worked, so I went ahead and gave it a shot. I picked up some tax forms and the instruction booklet. The very next day, I got started by opening and reading the instruction booklet, then going line by line until I finished preparing my taxes. I felt so accomplished—this was a big deal for me, as I was only 18 years old! I enjoyed figuring out how to increase my tax refund as much as possible. The process felt more like entertainment to me, as opposed to a burden.

So, I signed the tax form and mailed it off to the IRS. In about six weeks, I received my first refund check. Being so young, it felt wonderful, and the process really came easy for me. I felt like maybe I had a special talent for it, and I couldn't relate to why people hated doing their taxes so much—it just made sense to me. It was like a formula: you owe a large amount in taxes at first, then you take as many deductions as possible.

Later that fall, I enrolled in a junior college where I received a basketball scholarship and decided to take business and accounting classes. The first year, I prepared taxes for a couple of family members and a few college students who worked summer jobs and work-study jobs. My second year of school, my client list grew to sixteen college students and a few family members. At that time, I was only charging around $40, so I earned about $1200 in a few months. Of course, looking back, I know that I significantly undercharged for my services, but thankfully, now you can learn from my years of experience throughout this book.

After graduating from junior college, I needed to start earning some income. My girlfriend at the time was six months pregnant with our son, so I had to figure out a way to earn more. So, I started selling new cars and trucks at a Ford dealership. In my third year of selling new cars and trucks, I became the top salesman at our dealership and a top 500 salesperson in the nation. It was a great first job right after college, but it did not feel right for me long term.

Sure, I was earning a nice income of $60,000 to $70,000 a year, but I was missing life with my family by working 75 to 80 hours a week, including the holidays. The only days we got off were Thanksgiving, Christmas, and New Year's Day. So, we had good money coming in, but very little time to spend together as a family.

After seven consecutive years in the car business, I was getting a little burnt out and feeling like my life was not my *own*. If you have ever worked an unfulfilling job, you know how I felt: I was giving a lot of myself, but I wasn't gaining much in return. I made a good income, sure, but that is not enough when you really want to spend time with your family. Life isn't about making loads of money only to be too dead tired in the evenings to read a book to your children—a job should never take over your life! Instead, life is about work that makes you feel fulfilled while also enjoying some work/life balance.

One busy Saturday at work, I met a nice lady who was looking for a large SUV to use for work and family vacations. She mentioned that she needed legroom for her tall husband and three teenage kids. So, I showed her a few large SUVs and we began the test drive. While on the test drive, I asked her about her profession.

She mentioned that she had owned her own tax preparation business for the past six years. My interest was piqued, and I wanted to learn more about her clients and the income tax business because I was already preparing taxes for myself, as well as a few family members and friends. This is something I *knew* I was good at, but I hadn't thought that it would be possible to live off it. It was a good time to consider my options while seeking an exit from the long hours of the car business.

After the test drive, she decided that she liked the SUV and wanted to purchase it. So we started the credit application for financing. She mentioned that she was going to put down $30,000 and finance the rest. The beautiful white SUV had a retail price of $58,000, but after rebates and incentives, it came down to about $51,000. I asked her about her income to fill in the finance application, and she replied that she made $142,000 last year.

I was completely surprised—I had no idea how that was possible! So, I asked if she had any other jobs, considering tax season is typically from January to April. She replied that she didn't have any other jobs, and that was what her tax business generated in the four months, allowing her to have the rest of the year to herself and her family. To me, of course, this was an insight into what my life *could* be. I had the skills, I had the knowledge, and I even had a small client base... So why couldn't I become a tax person?

Once she purchased the vehicle, I thanked her for her business and asked for her business card. I guess this person was meant to be on my path! At that moment, I decided that I wanted to fully commit to becoming a tax preparer and start my own tax preparation business. It was something I was already doing as a side hustle to earn some extra cash, so I decided it was time to completely dedicate myself to it. If she could do it and then take the rest of the year off, then why couldn't I?

However, I knew I needed more training and knowledge about the tax business and to learn how to prepare more complex tax returns to provide greater value to the marketplace. I was working hard for my friends and family members, but this wasn't enough—I needed to know how a tax business works!

Over the next few weeks, it consumed my thoughts as I wondered how I could move forward and become a full-time tax preparer. So, I reached out to my client who owned the tax preparation business to express my interest in starting a tax business of my own. I asked if I could make an appointment to visit her office, observe her operations, and seek her guidance on how to get started. After our conversation, she advised me that the best way to begin and determine if I truly wanted to pursue this line of work was to take tax classes at one of the renowned tax firms.

One of the tax firms had a class starting in September that would meet on Tuesdays and Thursdays, from 5:00 to 6:00 p.m. I enrolled in the class and informed my boss at the dealership that I needed to attend therapy twice a week for my mental health, and I would take a late lunch on those days. I understand that it may seem like I lied to my boss, but to me, taking this class was a form of therapy because working at the car dealership was driving me crazy. I *genuinely* needed to take the class to learn the information for my mental well-being.

Once I completed my tax classes in December, I was offered a tax preparation job at the tax firm for the upcoming tax season. The hourly wage was only $10, but I needed to determine if this was the right career path for me. Thankfully, I had savings and had built up a six-month emergency fund in the bank to cover our living expenses, and my credit cards had zero balances. So, I had little to no debt. My wife and I made the decision to live with my parents for the next year or so.

Once I had made up my mind, I decided to fully commit to this new venture. There's a quote by Napoleon Hill that states, "Great achievement is usually born of great sacrifices and is never the result of selfishness." After a successful tax season with the renowned tax firm, I knew it was time to start my own tax business.

The next step was launching my own business. Since I was new to this venture, I wanted to start small with minimal overhead. I asked my wife's dad if I could use his home office since he was retired. I offered to pay him a monthly fee for using his office and to update the desk, chairs, and the outdated computer system he had. The best thing about his home office was that it was a separate room to the left of the front door to the house, providing privacy.

I started my tax business from this home office, and now my business is thriving! Throughout the years of experience I have acquired, I have gained specific expertise both in the field of tax preparation *and* in terms of creating a successful tax business. Entrepreneurship is not an easy road, but hopefully, with help from this book, you will be well on your way to creating your very own successful tax business too.

Throughout this book, we will cover every step you need to follow to launch a tax business from the ground up. Specifically, we will look at how you can do this from home, as a tax business doesn't require a brick-and-mortar office. This is perhaps one of the greatest aspects of the job—you get to work in your own home if you have the space, or you can lease a coworking space if you need a separate environment for your business.

We will be exploring key steps such as conducting market research, drafting a business plan, understanding tax laws and regulations, getting a tax certification and license, setting up your office, hiring and training a team (because chances are good you will need more people as your business grows!), how to price your services, how to *market* your services, how to build client relationships and retain clients, how to manage risk and legal considerations, and finally, how to grow and expand your business further.

The goal of this book is to give you an in-depth overview of the world of tax businesses so you can create your own without having to experience the same challenges I have had to face. I am thankful for the opportunity to meet someone who inspired me to take the leap and start my business, and hopefully, this book will be your incentive to do the same.

On that note, let's get started!

CHAPTER ONE

INTRODUCTION TO THE TAX INDUSTRY

Taxes aren't exactly *fun* for most people. In fact, to most, doing taxes and tax season are two of the things they fear when it rolls around each year! And yet, to someone who is *good* at doing taxes, this sector may be a great opportunity. In fact, in the world of finance and commerce, only a few sectors offer as rich and varied opportunities as the tax industry. You may be an aspiring tax consultant, or perhaps you have been working for a tax business and are now looking to launch your own. Regardless of where you are starting from, it is extremely important that you understand the fundamentals of tax law and consulting before you dive deeper.

Taxes: They Are Here to Stay!

See, taxes are an inherent part of any economy. They are the lifeblood of government revenue, and they are what facilitates public spending and societal development. They are something people often complain about, especially those who feel they are paying too much. This, in a way, can be a great selling point for your services—people like to get money back, and you can help them do so! As a tax professional, you get to help people who are trying to navigate the intricacies of tax regulations and obligations, and you are able to guide them through this process, making it simpler, easier, and more enjoyable for them. You are the one in charge of *demystifying* complex tax laws that only a few understand, and you can help your clients meet their legal obligations while reducing their tax burden. The greatest part of all this? Taxes will never disappear—you will *always* need to pay taxes, and so will others, meaning that your job is secure.

What Does a Tax Professional Do?

Your job as a professional in the tax industry goes beyond filing forms and helping clients get significant tax returns. You also play the role of a navigator, whereby you are guiding your clients through the confusing maze of tax law with precision and insight. Your duties will vary depending on the kind of tax services you offer, but at its core, your role is to ensure accuracy, legality, and efficiency in all tax-related matters.

There are four key roles you will likely be playing. First, there is that of the **advisor**, where you provide strategic advice to your clients based on the tax issues they are facing. You help your clients understand and navigate complex tax laws and regulations by applying them to their specific case. This helps them make decisions that align with their financial goals. This also involves staying on top of the latest changes in tax codes, identifying areas where clients could be saving on taxes, and advising on the tax implications that certain significant financial decisions will involve, such as when they invest in property or are interested in expanding their business (among other examples).

You are also a **preparer**, which is perhaps the part of the job you know best. Here, you are responsible for preparing accurate and compliant tax returns for your clients. This is where your eye for detail is crucial, as you need to have both a deep understanding of tax laws and regulations and must know how to sift through financial documents efficiently. You will need to calculate tax liabilities and fill out the appropriate tax forms. Then, you will need to ensure that tax return forms are filed by the right deadlines, so you help your clients avoid penalties and late fees.

You also work as a **representative** on behalf of your clients when dealing with tax authorities. This may involve communicating with tax agencies regarding audits, disputes, notices, and the like. You may also represent a client in tax court or during an audit, helping to defend your client's position or negotiate a favorable outcome on their behalf.

And finally, you work as an **educator**. The tax industry is intimidating for many people because of its complex nature. Taxes are also scary for some as the result of not paying them can mean jail time in the worst-case scenario. Therefore, your job is also to impart your knowledge to clients so you help them understand the complexities of their taxes, the tax codes that apply to their finances, and the implications of these. This role therefore is about more than just sharing simple information, but also *empowering* them so they can make the right decisions. You may need to explain the nuances of tax credits and deductions, outline tax implications of life changes (e.g., marriage, retirement), or teach a new business owner how to provide quarterly tax information.

These roles require a *unique* blend of skills and competencies that only a few truly have! Therefore, this is a job that requires you to be interested in the field, and interested in helping others gain better insights into their spending habits.

Different Sectors within the Tax Industry

Tax businesses do not necessarily only serve individuals or small businesses. There are many tax sectors, all of which you can consider before you decide which one to specialize in. Of course, you can also offer a variety of tax services, although you may benefit from getting help from other experts in this field by scaling up your business and hiring experts for each sector. This, however, is something you can consider down the line.

First, there is the obvious **individual income tax sector**. This is primarily concerned with taxing *personal income*, whereby you assist your clients in preparing and filing their annual tax returns, advise them on deductions and credits, and strategize tax-savings measures. For this, you will need a comprehensive understanding of tax brackets, file statuses, capital gains taxes, and so on.

Second, there is the **business tax sector**. This is where you work with businesses—both small and large—and advise them on tax matters that affect their operations. Here, you may need to prepare and file corporate tax returns, structure transactions for tax efficiency, handle payroll taxes, advise on the tax implications of business decisions such as mergers, investments, or acquisitions, and so on. Currently, it is becoming increasingly easy to launch a business, with people creating LLCs left and right. This means that you are very likely to find many clients looking for advisory services before they get started so they can be sure to abide by the laws and regulations they need to understand and respect.

Third, you may be interested in **international taxes**. We live in an increasingly inter-connected world as globalization has made the trading of items much more efficient.

Therefore, as a tax professional in this sector, you will be dealing with complex tax issues that have to do with cross-border activities. In this role, your job is to help your clients understand and navigate multinational tax laws, transfer pricing, tax treaties, foreign tax credits, and many more similar concepts, so they can be sure to abide by the laws and regulations in place. Of course, you will also need to optimize global tax liabilities.

There are other sectors you may be interested in including **estate and gift tax**, which is a niche sector that focuses on the taxation of estates and gifts, such as when homes are transferred as inheritance. **Sales and use tax**, which relates to the imposed taxes on the sale or lease of goods and services, may also be a sector you are interested in, while **property tax, nonprofit tax, and excise tax** are all also options.

Preparing Yourself and Staying Informed

To truly understand the tax industry, you will need to immerse yourself in the evolving landscape of local, national, and perhaps even international tax regulations (depending on your preference). You will have to understand the different tax obligations depending on your clients' income brackets, and will need to have a comprehensive understanding of business tax requirements too. Importantly, you will have to stay on top of ongoing changes in tax legislation, as a small change in the law can lead to a significant impact on your clients' tax returns. As a tax professional, your job is to provide great advice to your clients, to facilitate tax planning, compliance, and risk mitigation, and most importantly, to always ensure your clients are satisfied!

Why Start a Tax Business?

If you are in between jobs, or have been working for a tax business as a consultant, you may be wondering why you should switch over to the world of entrepreneurship and launch your own venture. There are many potential opportunities. For example, one is that businesses of all sizes—from ambitious startups to multinational conglomerates—require tax consultation services to ensure that their tax obligations are fulfilled. On top of this, you of course also have individuals who are always looking for professional help to understand and manage their taxes, especially as their financial affairs become increasingly complex. Every fiscal year brings a surge in demand for tax services, especially as businesses and individuals alike rush to file their tax returns. Indeed, the resilience of a tax business is one of its greatest appeals—you will never be out of a job, even despite the recent advances in AI!

Where Does the Tax Industry Stand Today?

Speaking of AI, let's consider where the industry currently stands. There are current trends reflecting quite the dynamic shift in the way tax services are being delivered. For example, as we increasingly embrace digital culture, online tax consulting platforms are becoming more and more popular, whereby they offer remote and on demand services to clients all over the world. Similarly, AI and machine learning tools are changing the game, as they enhance accuracy, efficiency, and allow us to provide more personalized services to our clients. While AI may be scary to some, it is not something to be wary about, but rather is something we should see as a tool, allowing us to provide better services and to do so more efficiently with the help of tech.

In fact, the rise of AI is sometimes seen as something that is threatening jobs in the industry, but it's important to acknowledge that technology does not undermine the value of personalized customer service and professional expertise. Tax laws are complex and continue to grow in complexity, and while software *can* handle the most time-consuming aspects of many processes we take care of as tax experts, it is *we* who bring this personal touch to the process and who bring our experience-based insights and customized advice. This is irreplaceable by any machine! This means that there is a growing demand for tax professionals who can *blend* technological proficiency with human prowess, thereby offering a comprehensive service that unites convenience and expertise.

Where Is the Tax Industry Headed?

In terms of prospects for your business, the tax industry is likely to continue growing at a rapid pace. Creating a business has never been easier, which means that tax professionals are increasingly called on to help those launching businesses to fulfill their tax requirements. The industry will furthermore continue to be shaped by regulatory changes, economic developments, as well as technological advancements, which will require tax professionals like you to remain agile, ready-to-learn, and adaptable. In fact, if you have been working in the industry for a few years now and are considering launching your own tax business, now is the time to take a moment and consider the set of skills that you have.

Are you up-to-date with the skills needed to remain relevant? Do you need to update or expand your skills to remain as efficient as you can be in this field given the new available technology?

Starting a tax business is not just about spotting a profitable opportunity, but about embracing an industry that is both challenging *and* rewarding. If you are someone who enjoys staying current on the complexities and constant changes in the tax laws and regulations, you have a great opportunity to provide valuable services to help other people maintain their financial safety and security. You can make a difference, one tax return at a time, and help clients who may be overwhelmed by their fiscal responsibilities, while also helping them gain more insights into their financial health and prosperity. Having a tax expert available to help them can be a life-changing experience for individual tax payers and business owners as it helps them feel more in control of their finances and can also give them the peace of mind they've wanted for a long time! So, your job as a tax business owner is not only to provide clients with expertise and skill, but to do so with passion and the commitment to serving your clients with integrity, care, and proficiency.

A passion for working in the tax industry is essential before you launch a business. Since you're reading this book, I assume that this is indeed the case. Now, we are now ready to head over to the first step for launching your own business, which is to research the competition.

CHAPTER TWO

CONDUCTING MARKET RESEARCH

In chapter one, we explored the various tax sectors that you may be interested in. Although starting with the sector you are most experienced in or interested in is one approach, it is also important to consider whether there is demand for your services. After all, this is a business like any other, meaning that you need to ensure that there is demand for the services you are offering before jumping head-first into the process of launching your new venture. This is called *market research*, and it is like a compass that guides your strategic planning. It allows you to identify opportunities, understand your competition, recognize your potential clients, and position your business for success. Throughout this chapter, we will explore exactly how to do this.

Identifying Your Competitors

We will begin with the **competitor analysis** part of market research. When stepping into the business landscape of providing tax services, we need to consider who you are going up against. The good news is that many people need tax services, meaning that you will not struggle significantly to find clients. However, to position yourself as a tax expert without getting lost in the masses of other experts and losing your unique touch, you need to know what others are offering to showcase how *you* are different. You are entering an area where many players coexist—they range from small to large firms, to independent tax consultants, to tech-driven tax software. The better you understand what they are offering, the better you can learn from their operations and position yourself as an expert in your field who's offering something completely different.

Start by creating a list of **potential competitors**, such as direct ones (e.g., those offering the same or similar tax services as you are planning to offer) and indirect ones (those offering alternative solutions to similar problems faced by your potential clients). For example, a tax software program, as an *alternative* solution to hiring a tax consultant, might not offer the same product you can as it is not a personalized consultation, but it still addresses the same need that your potential clients are looking to fulfill, namely helping clients file taxes. On the other hand, your direct competitors will include the people who are also working as tax consultants in your area. Create a list that includes both broad *and* specific competitors, such as local tax consultants, and other tax businesses on the regional, local, and national level, as taxes can be done remotely and hence your competitors aren't limited to the ones near you!

You then want to **analyze what your competition is offering**. For example, you will want to look at the kinds of services they are providing, who their target audience is, as well as their pricing models. Some of these competitors may offer individual tax returns, and others may offer corporate tax services. Some will also offer a blend of services. Look at their niches—are they mainly offering international tax services? Corporate tax services? Are they solely working with individuals? The goal is to pinpoint a *gap* in the market. The more you understand what others are offering, the more you can identify these gaps and create a business offering that serves these needs.

You should also pay attention to your competitors' **marketing strategies**, namely how their potential clients find them. How do they market themselves? What channels do they use? Do they primarily rely on traditional marketing methods, such as referrals (which I started out with since I worked for my friends and family), or are they also using more modern digital marketing techniques, such as marketing their services on social media, using content marketing, and search engine optimization? Doing this research can teach you about the kinds of tactics that work well in your industry, as well as identify which ones are not currently being used and where you may be able to gain a certain advantage.

Then, study their **unique selling proposition (USP)**. This is the proposition that entices clients to work with them instead of other service providers. This USP is the factor that makes them a more interesting partner to work with than other competitors. This is also something you will need to come up with! A USP may be something such as extensive experience, a wide range of services, affordable pricing, exceptional customer service, or maybe the use of advanced technology. The more you know about competitors' USPs, the more you can understand what clients in your chosen niche value, and hence, what *you* need to implement to distinguish yourself from the competition.

Finally, you will want to track their **reviews and reputation**. A lot can be read between the lines of a review—a happy customer will leave a great review, but an unhappy customer will most likely leave a very detailed account of their experience to warn others. This is information you can use to learn more about what customers expect in terms of services. You can check online reviews, client testimonials, as well as any news articles or press releases. What are their clients saying? What kinds of strengths and weaknesses do they seem to have? If a similar pain point keeps emerging from reviews, you can tailor your services to address them.

Please keep in mind that you should not use your competitor analysis to mimic others' services or business models, but rather to learn about the industry and to find the gaps in the current market. You should be creating a unique brand and offering services that utilize your skills and meet the needs of your prospective clients, and this is where analyzing what's missing can come in handy.

Recognizing Your Potential Clients

You have identified who your competition is—now is the time to identify your potential clients. In the tax industry, you need to understand your clients very well as they will be the primary source of revenue and hence the lifeblood of your business. This is not unlike other kinds of businesses, but in the tax industry, this is even more important, namely because your clients will come to you for advice and support. Hence, for clients to choose to work with you, you must be ready to put your clients first and to demonstrate that you care deeply about their financial well-being. Whether we like it or not, money does impact our happiness, and therefore, working with a tax professional is a big leap of faith for many. Your clients want to know that you care about them and that you are personally committed to helping them to keep as much of their earnings as possible at tax time. To do this, you need to know who you are targeting very specifically. This means you must take the time to understand their specific needs and then develop a plan that best serves them.

First, let's **identify potential clients.** Your clients can be individuals or businesses, and they will each have a unique set of needs and challenges for you to help them address. For example, individual clients may need your help with personal income tax, with tax disputes, or with estate and gift tax, while businesses are more likely to require services related to payroll, sales, or corporate tax—or international tax issues.

You will therefore need to **segment** your client base based on factors such as income level, industry, geographical location, or perhaps by life events. You could, for example, target self-employed individuals, small businesses, or individuals with a high income, while you may also want to work with recently married couples who need help figuring out their taxes. The key is to define exactly who your potential clients are based on the kinds of services you plan to offer as well as your expertise.

Next, create a client persona. This can be very helpful to better understand your clients. This persona is a fictional representation of your ideal client. This involves having de-tailed demographic information on them, as well as some information on their financial situation and an understanding of their main pain points. For example, let's consider a client persona for your business who we'll call "Self-Employed Sam." This persona is a thirty-year-old, freelance graphic designer, who does not quite understand how to do taxes as a self-employed person. Otherwise, you might have "Entrepreneur Emily," a forty-year-old woman who owns a small e-commerce business and who needs help with corporate and sales taxes. Creating these personas helps you pinpoint and visualize who you are targeting as a client, which can then make it easier to figure out how you can win them as clients using marketing strategies we'll discuss later in the book. The key is to understand their pain points so you can tailor your services to help resolve them.

This indeed means that your next goal is to **understand your clients' needs**. You have a potential client in mind and have created a few client personas—now, identify how this information translates into identifying their needs and how you can help them. What kind of tax challenges are they facing? What services might they look for from a tax professional? Consider the expectations they may have for the services you offer and how quickly they can expect delivery, customer service and how to contact you, as well as the range of prices you charge. This is information you can gather through market research, such as by using surveys or conducting interviews. However, you can also search online for this—look at sites such as Reddit, as you may be able to find threads where people are discussing their tax issues. Social media may also be a good source of information as potential clients may be discussing their key issues there.

The final step is to **build services around your clients' needs and wants**. Here, you need to make sure you are offering services that address their pain points. The service *offering, pricing strategy, and marketing approach* will **all** depend on the kinds of pain points your targeted clients are looking to solve. So, your business processes and services each need to be carefully designed to meet your clients' needs and to exceed their expectations!

Understanding Local, Regional, and National Market Trends

Importantly, you also need to know what the trends are locally, regionally, and nationally. As mentioned earlier, when I sold the SUV to the client who owns her own tax business, I was surprised to hear that she could make over $140,000 a year because peak tax season is between January and April. However, your services will also most likely be required at other times, such as when clients need your advice and consultancy services.

In your search, start by looking at **local market trends**. At this level, focus on the economic conditions and the specific tax regulations in your area. If you live in a city with a growing number of startups, you may be able to predict an increasing demand for tax services relating to small businesses. Likewise, learning about local tax laws may be a great strategic move to help residents who might need your expertise to comply with these regulations. Locally, you also need to consider the socio-economic demographic. If you are in a high-income area, chances are your clients will need more assistance with tax planning and wealth management. On the other hand, potential clients in an area with a lower income bracket will need affordable tax preparation services and won't typically require more complex services.

Make sure to also consider **regional market trends**. At the regional level, you may want to consider, for example, more extensive economic and regulatory trends. In a community that is home to mainly manufacturing industries, you will most likely see greater demand for corporate tax services. If this region has generous tax incentives for renewable energy, you might find that there is a market for these tax services. Similarly, if you notice a change in regional tax laws, you may see that new opportunities arise. New tax incentives aimed at boosting business outcomes can create an opportunity to market your consultancy services to businesses who may be interested in figuring out how they can benefit from the changes.

On a **national scale**, trends in the economy can also positively or negatively affect your business. In an economic downturn, businesses might seek out your services to help identify cost-saving avenues they can explore. On the other hand, individuals who normally use your services may no longer be able to afford them if they are trying to reduce their own costs. On the other hand, in an economic upturn, individuals may need more help to figure out how to manage their increased income and investments.

Finally, do not underestimate the role of **socio-cultural trends!** For example, consider the change that the Covid-19 pandemic brought to the way we work. A few years ago, hybrid work was completely new and, in fact, rare! Nowadays, employees expect that companies will allow them to work from home at least one day a week. This shift has the potential to change the way taxes work too, as more and more individuals are choosing to become freelancers or digital nomads—two categories that often greatly benefit from accessing tax services.

Conduct a SWOT Analysis

A SWOT analysis is a tool you can use to perform strategic planning. This is an acronym that stands for Strengths, Weaknesses, Opportunities, and Threats. This is a great way to evaluate the internal and external aspects of your business, which will provide you with the insights you need to create effective strategies that work well for your tax business.

First, you need to identify **strengths**, which are the *internal positive attributes* of your business. These set you apart from your competition. For example, you might have a team of professionals to help you meet clients' needs, or you might have specific knowledge and experience in a niche area, such as international tax law, based on years of experience. You may have also built great relationships in your local community, or you may have developed a unique way to prepare taxes. Think about what you do very well, the resources you have, and what others see as your strengths. For example, I am known as "The Refund

Man" by my close friends and family, as they received larger tax refunds based on my tax assistance. If you have experience in the field, consider the compliments and feedback you have received—what are you known for? Consider other factors too, such as your skills, your knowledge, your network, or the unique assets you have to offer. These can be used to make yourself stand out from the competition!

Second, look for your **weaknesses**. We all have them. These are factors that your business may need help or support with due to limitations in your knowledge or skill-set. For example, if you are working with a team, as individuals or as a group, it may lack experience in certain areas. Or maybe, you are not as technologically adept as your competitors. You may also have a limited marketing budget, or may only have a small amount to start your business with (as I did—but it did not hold me back!). The idea is that by identifying your weaknesses, you can also find solutions to them. For example, my small starting budget led me to use my father in law's home office to cut down on costs. However, I did not let it stop me from going for it and getting started. You should be honest and realistic about your weaknesses, as not doing so only hinders your capacity to address them and overcome them.

Third, **spot the opportunities**. These are the external factors in your business environment that will give you the competitive edge you need to find clients despite having competitors around you. This may be based on market trends, as discussed earlier, or may result from changes in regulations, such as new tax laws that can lead businesses to seek out your consultancy services to see how they can benefit. There may be a shift in customer needs, or technological advancements that you can take advantage of. Ideally, you will think about how your strengths align with these arising opportunities, and then how you can use them to grow and expand your business further. Capitalize on the *external* business landscape while using your *internal* assets.

Fourth and finally, **evaluate potential threats.** Your business will face threats—there is no doubt about it. You might have a growing number of competitors, there may be changes in tax laws that disadvantage you, there may be an economic downturn, or negative shifts in market trends. For example, we are facing more and more technological advances which, while they can lead to improvements and help you be more efficient, they will nonetheless affect tax services. You should know how to pivot and use them to your advantage!

With the market analysis complete, you are ready to start working on building your business. You know what else is out there and which kinds of clients you want to work with. You have an idea of the services you *can* offer and which ones you would like to focus on first. Next up, it's time to combine all this information, as well as your strategy, into a well-organized business plan.

CHAPTER THREE

DRAFTING A BUSINESS PLAN

The business plan you create will be the document that you can return to whenever you feel that you need to realign with your business vision. Initially, it serves as a way for you to map out your business idea, team, strategy, services, and marketing strategy. Therefore, it is an important document that you should spend some time working on. Thankfully, you've already completed one of the most important parts of the business plan: the market analysis. The remainder, however, still needs to be created.

Executive Summary

The first part of the business plan is the executive summary. This part of the plan is where you encapsulate the essence of your tax business. You should provide a high-level view of your strategies, goals, and the unique value that your services will bring to the market. This should be compelling and convincing, and it should act as a snapshot of your business. The goal is to convince readers (who will read it in the future if you choose to seek funding to expand and scale your business) that your business model is viable and that it will be successful.

For example, let's imagine that your envisioned business is a comprehensive tax services firm that aspires to simplify the complex world of taxes for individuals and businesses alike. You are seeking to fill the gap in the market by offering personalized, reliable, and accessible tax services that cater to a diverse client base ranging from individuals to small and medium-sized enterprises. It should include information on your mission, your vision, your core values, your offering (i.e., services), your awareness of the industry and its rapidly changing nature, information on why your business is going to grow and be successful, and information on how you plan to market your services. Think of it as an elevator pitch.

The executive summary can be used to pitch your company to others, but it also serves as a great way for you to evaluate whether your business idea will be valuable to your target clients. You can use it to determine your mission, vision, values, and how you will approach different processes such as the marketing strategy. If you do not want to formulate an entire business plan from scratch, just writing up an executive summary can also be a great place to start to gauge whether your idea is viable!

Company Description

Next up, you will need a company description. This is where you will include a detailed introduction to your business. This should showcase a clear understanding of what your business is all about, namely what it does, who it serves, and what makes it equipped to succeed. The company description needs to have a few key points, such as the **business name and legal structure.** This is where you state the legal name of the business (based on how you have registered it) and the structure you have chosen to use. You can, for example, set it up as a sole proprietorship, a partnership, a limited liability company, or a corporation. This will impact your taxes, personal liability, and even your day-to-day operations, so make sure that this is clearly identified.

Then, you describe the **nature** of the business, which is what it does. For example, you can describe the range of services that it offers, such as tax preparation, planning, consulting, as well as resolution services. You should be explicitly clear about the nature of the services, namely by outlining how they will be meeting your clients' needs. Next up, consider the **industry and market** you are targeting. You are working in the context of a specific industry, so you should mention this. Make sure you know the industry's size, its growth rate, and its major trends. You can also mention the specific market segment you are targeting, such as individuals, small businesses, corporations, or a more specific niche.

Then comes the **value proposition**. This is arguably the most important part of the description as this is where you determine *why* your business is *unique* in the way it meets the needs of its target market. Are you filling a gap in the market? Are you offering unique expertise? Are you offering affordable services for a community who isn't currently being served in your area? This is where you truly distinguish yourself, and this is based on market analysis, which we explored in the first chapter.

Finally, if you are planning to show this plan to investors later, include a **business location**. If, on the other hand, you will be conducting your business solely online, you should make sure to explain how this can and will affect your services—this is a good time to start considering how you can make the most out of working online, and what challenges you might face compared to brick-and-mortar companies.

The next section of the business plan is the market analysis, which we have already explored in detail. So let's jump right to the next section, which is organization and management.

Organization and Management

This section of the business plan is where you start looking at the *structure* behind your business. This will depend on whether you want to work as an independent tax expert, or whether you want to hire a team of experts who each specialize in a different tax sector. If you have a team, you will want to outline who they are, what their roles are, and the experience and expertise they each bring to the business (this aspect is primarily needed if you will show the plan to an investor). You can also include any roles and responsibilities that will be added in the future.

Services, Marketing, and Sales

The next two sections are the **services and products** you will offer, as well as the **marketing and sales strategy** you will adopt. First you need to outline the tax services your business will offer in great detail. Explain what the benefits are to each of these, as well as how they compare to competitors' offerings. Here, you need to be explicit and explain *exactly* what you will be offering—remember, this business plan serves as your guidelines and steps to follow when the time comes to set things in motion. The clearer you are in your business plan, the easier it will be later to implement.

Then, the **marketing and sales** strategy is where you begin to outline how you will attract clients. Will you use online marketing tools? Will you look for clients in your local area, starting with your family and friends? Starting with people close to you is a great approach as they can vouch for you to others as well, providing you with quite a list of clients within just a few weeks, or even days!

Funding Requests and Financial Projections

Finally, if you plan to reach out to investors, you will also need to include information regarding the funding you are looking for. Whether or not you will be seeking funding, you should include a financial projection where you gauge your projected income, cash flow, and balance sheets for the next three to five years. These can be estimated based on your market analysis and how you intend to price your services (again, this is something that you can gauge based on your market analysis).

And just like that, you have a business plan! If you are indeed planning to show it to investors, make sure that you are ready to provide a lot of data to back up what you are saying. If you are discussing tremendous growth forecasts in the industry, have the data to back it up. If your unique selling proposition is based on observations, do some more research to find data that will back it up.

Once your business plan is set up, it is time to start thinking about your licenses and certifications.

CHAPTER FOUR

TAX CERTIFICATION AND LICENSES

With a sturdy business plan in hand, we are ready for the next step, which is to consider the certification and licenses you will need to be considered a tax expert. In any professional field, you need to have the right credentials to be considered both an expert and reliable as a service provider. In the tax industry specifically, your clients are entrusting you with their sensitive financial information and their tax obligations, meaning that they are relying on you to ensure their financial well-being. To this end, you need to secure the right certifications and licenses, not only so you operate within the legal guidelines, but to showcase that you are committed to being a professional and to providing excellent and ethical work!

Your Tax Certifications: More

than

Just a

Certificate

The tax certification you receive from the IRS, called a Preparer Tax Identification Number (PTIN) is more than a paper certificate. It certifies that you are trained and authorized to legally work as a Tax Preparer. Although the IRS does not require applicants to have any specific training or licenses to open a tax business, it is nonetheless a great way to add to your credibility. For example, you can choose to enroll in the IRS Annual Filing Season Program (AFSP), to learn more about federal tax law. This is an 18-hour continuing education and training program. Upon completion, you will earn a certificate as proof of competence which adds to your credibility as a tax preparation expert. You will also be listed in the IRS Directory of Federal Tax Return Preparers. Consider getting additional training and credentials such as Certified Public Accountant or an Enrolled Agent to again boost your credibility in the eyes of your clients.

These licenses are especially important to show that you abide by an **ethical code of conduct** as a tax expert.

CHAPTER FIVE

SETTING UP YOUR OFFICE, AND GETTING STARTED!

You have your licenses and certifications, so you are all set to get to work! Before you can create your business website and implement your marketing strategies, you will need to have a **space to work**. Thankfully, in 2023, we cancan work from anywhere! As I did by working in a home office, you can create your very own home office too, if you have some space in your home where you can fit a desk and a few office machines and supplies.

A Home Office or Coworking?

Personally, I started my business as simply and inexpensively as possible, as we were living on the savings in an emergency fund during those few months. So, I decided to work primarily from home. Working solely from home is not for everyone. It can be very distracting to be surrounded by your home environment, especially if you do not have the discipline to stay focused (or have ADHD!). Going to a coworking space can be a great help as it can provide a different setting for you to work, without the stress and pressure of not feeling productive because you are at home. That being said, coworking offices can be costly—it depends on how much you are willing to invest in your business when you are just starting out.

What You Will Need

For now, we will assume that you are working from home. To get started, you will need a few essential items. This includes, for example, IRS forms, a reliable and efficient desktop computer and/or a laptop with anti-malware as well as anti-virus software, as you do not want your clients' personal data being leaked and or accessed by people who should not have access to it. You will, of course, need a reliable internet connection, as well as professional tax preparation software. Then, make sure to acquire basic office supplies, such as paper, pens, notebooks, staplers, binders, and so on. Necessary office equipment will include a scanner, fax machine, and a printer. Then, you will want to print out some business cards and marketing materials. You will need to have filing cabinets to store tax records. These need to be kept for a minimum of **three years**.

You must have a dedicated home office space and create an environment you find conducive to getting work done that is also set up to welcome clients. We *need* a space that is dedicated to our work and separate from where we live, as otherwise, we will simply struggle to feel motivated to get any work done! We are all guilty of it—the couch often seems to be a much more comfortable place to get work done than the office! So, make your office comfortable. Get an ergonomic chair that feels comfortable and is supportive for your back, a footrest if it helps your posture, and make sure that your desk and chair are set up so you are sitting with your elbows at a ninety-degree angle when your hands are on your keyboard to avoid any wrist injuries.

Obtain Your PTIN

Next, it's time to get your PTIN. This is done by applying online on the IRS website. You will need to provide information such as your social security number, your name, address, and birth date, as well as your individual tax returns from the previous year. If you have any felony convictions, or if you have had any issues with taxes in the past—whether business-related or personal—you will have to explain these to the IRS. Then, when you *renew* it, you will also have to supply more information. The process is very simple, you just need to create an account, apply for it, pay the fee, and receive your number.

Choosing a Name for Your Business

Now it's time to consider the name you will choose for your business. This name is extremely important! It is the very first impression that you are making on your potential customers, potential partners, and even investors if you choose that route. This name sets the tone for all your interactions, meaning that it needs to represent the image you want to project for your business. It is essential to choose a name that conveys your business identity and its value proposition which you have defined in the previous chapters. This name should be distinctive, memorable, and it should hold meaning, so your prospective clients immediately know what to expect from your business and services.

To choose the best possible name, you first must **understand your business**. As we've seen, your business is a combination of what you offer, who your clients are, and how you differ from the competition. The name therefore needs to encapsulate this, as well as its vision, its mission, its value proposition, and the unique selling point—all elements that have developed while creating a business plan. Begin by **brainstorming ideas**. Make a list and be open to all the possibilities—focus on quantity instead of quality. Write down any name that comes to your mind, even if it is very outlandish! You never know what *might* sound bizarre at first, only to realize that it indeed sounds great. Use techniques such as online name generators, mind mapping, or AI! Why not ask ChatGPT for some help with this?

Next, you can start **shortlisting names**. Look at names that are easy to pronounce and to spell. Keep it memorable, and especially *relevant* to your business and industry, as well as the tax sector you are in. You should avoid names that could limit your growth and scaling efforts, or that are far too generic—you need to think in terms of search engine optimization. You can always ask for help with this step, and in fact, asking for feedback from others is a great way to gauge whether the names you have come up with are indeed good candidates or whether you need to do a bit more work. Keep this rule of thumb in mind as you are considering potential business names: it should be easy to communicate it clearly over the phone even with a bad connection. If you need to repeat it many times, or if you need to spell it out for people to understand, consider changing the name to something that is simpler and easier to grasp.

Once you've got a short list of options, you will need to check them for availability. This is an important step to take *before* you get attached to the name, specifically because you may end up feeling like the name you've chosen is perfect for you, only to find out that it is already taken. So, make sure that the name you want for your business is **available for use**. To do this, check whether the name is already trademarked, or whether another business is already using it. You can check on the Internet quickly, but you should also check the US Patent and Trademark Office's database as well as your state's business registry. Besides the legal aspects, you also need to check the Internet to see if the business name you've chosen already has a **digital presence**. After all, we live in an increasingly interconnected world, so you will need to make sure the website domain is not already in use. Check all kinds of domain registrars, or conduct a simple web search. If your exact business name is not available as a .com domain, don't be discouraged. Consider other suitable domain extensions like .net, .biz, .co, or even more specific ones like. tax if possible. You will also need to check whether your business name is available on social media platforms. Social media is becoming an increasingly important marketing tool, so you will want to make sure that your business name (or a very close variant) can be used as your handle across these platforms. *Consistency* is important with your business name, especially as your online presence can significantly enhance your brand's recognition. Not only this, but make sure that your brand name isn't associated with any other kind of name, business, or brand that could tarnish your own reputation. Finally, checking availability doesn't stop at the business, domain, and social media names. It extends to the **visual branding elements** as well! Think about the following: are there logos remarkably like what you envisioned for your business? If so, you might need to rethink your plans to avoid branding confusion, and to make sure that you stand out as a new business on the market. Choosing your business name may sound very complex and time consuming, but don't worry—it will work out! Yes, it might feel tedious at first, but the goal is to have a business name that *truly belongs to you*, both legally and digitally. Once you have that unique and unclaimed name that perfectly represents your business, you will know it was well worth the effort!

Now, it's time to do your final evaluation and to choose exactly which name you want. Here, you will want to thoughtfully review each potential name, and assess it against key criteria. Gauge each name's overall fit for your business. Be as objective as possible, but also allow your intuition to play a part. Throughout the process, ask yourself some critical questions. Does the name reflect your business's identity and values? Is it relevant to your industry and services? Does it resonate with your target market, and does it have the potential to stand out in the crowded marketplace? Does it lend itself well to visual representation, such as a logo or website design? Importantly, **can you see the name scaling as your business grows and potentially diversifies its services?** Sure, you might be in the tax business, but you might also end up offering other kinds of services down the line if you become interested in other subcategories, like financial planning services. This is also where you can ask for other people's feedback. For example, you can start by sharing your shortlisted names with your colleagues, your mentors, friends, potential clients, and the like. This feedback might be hard to hear (especially if you have landed on a name that you really like, only to receive negative feedback on that name from others), but it can nonetheless shed new light on this process and highlight potential advantages or issues that you might not have considered before. You could also run a small focus group or an online poll so you can gather a wider range of opinions. In the end, however, the decision is completely yours! Your new name *must* resonate with you on a personal level, and it needs to align with *your* vision for the business. So, if the feedback helps, great! If not, that's okay too, if you feel confident with your decision.

Registering Your Business

Once you've decided on the name for your business, the next essential step is registering it. Now, you might ask, "Why do I have to register the name?" Well, registering your business name secures it legally and affirms your ownership rights, meaning that others cannot use it to start their own business. It protects your business from name disputes and grants you exclusive use within your state (it could be done at the national level too, but it may make more sense to start out at the state level before you branch out, unless you are planning to expand your business nationally soon). However, remember that this process may vary depending on your area, so make sure that you understand your specific state's rules and regulations before you start the registration process. Otherwise, you might be missing essential documents when you have your appointment to register your business name!

Initiating the registration process will usually involve filing with the Secretary of State's office in your state, or a similar business authority, depending on where you are located and what the local authorities are. However, don't jump in without researching the process first! Each state has unique regulations, so familiarize yourself with them before proceeding to make sure that you are not wasting your time by showing up to a meeting unprepared, or by trying to register a business without all the necessary documents. Usually, states will offer two primary methods for registering your business name: registering a **Doing Business As** (DBA) or establishing a business structure like a **Limited Liability Company** (LLC) or a corporation (something we will discuss shortly).

On the other hand, if you're going into the tax industry as a sole proprietor (where you are the sole owner of your business, and hence are also liable for it), you might use your legal name for your business. But if you opt for a more distinctive business name, you need to register a **DBA**. This DBA, which works as a fictitious business name, is important for you to be able to open business bank accounts, accept payments, and to demonstrate overall clarity about who is behind the business.

On the other hand, if you plan to form a partnership, LLC, or corporation, the registration of your business name is *integrated* into the business formation process, so your business name will get registered when you file your business formation documents, meaning that you don't need to do it twice!

Please remember that **a registered business name does not *equate* to a trademark**. It's true that registering your business name does provide *some* level of protection, but it is limited to your *state*, so it does not protect you completely! If you want to protect your business name *nationally*, you will need to register a trademark with the United States Patent and Trademark Office (USPTO). However, this is a lot more complex, and it requires much more investment in terms of time and money (though it is useful if you plan to start a business that expands and scales nationally over time!).

Choosing the Legal Structure

Considering that you have chosen to start a tax business, chances are that you understand the tax implications of a sole proprietorship over those of an LLC quite well. That being said, it is not *always* the case! In fact, you may not have any idea of where or how to start, and/or of the tax implications of various business structures (in which case you will need to undergo training on taxes as this is a crucial aspect of tax preparation for many individuals and businesses alike!).

Choosing the legal structure for your business is a crucial step, not just a bureaucratic box to check off. It's a decision that will have lasting implications on how you operate your business, the taxes you'll pay, and your personal liability. So, let's start by debunking what this legal structure refers to. Simply explained, the legal structure you choose will determine the legal framework within which your business operates. This choice shapes the rights and responsibilities for your business, including its liability and tax obligations, and how profits and losses will be distributed (if you end up having people working for you, or if you have an LLC with many members).

Once this is clear, we can start considering the four main types of business structures to consider: Sole Proprietorship, Partnership, Corporation, and Limited Liability Company (LLC).

As a **Sole Proprietorship**, you're the *sole* owner of the business, and there's no legal distinction between you and your business. This simplicity makes it an attractive option for many solo entrepreneurs (because it means less paperwork). However, it also means you're personally liable for all business debts and obligations. So, if you end up in debt, or if your business fails, you are liable for much more than you are liable for as a limited liability company (LLC). This can also have rather serious repercussions on your credit score, for example, if you need to declare bankruptcy.

Next, a **Partnership**, which can be either general or limited, means the business is owned and operated by two or more individuals. It's true that partnerships mean more resources, but they *also* introduce *shared liability*. Remember, "two heads are better than one" comes with its challenges too. And here's an important one: don't go into business with a friend unless you have experience working on a business idea together. This can be catastrophic, and it can also seriously hurt your reputation as a business owner if the business is in your name.

Corporations, which are also known as C corporations, are more complex in nature. They are *separate legal entities* owned by shareholders, meaning the corporation itself, **not** the shareholders, is legally liable for the actions and the debts that the business incurs. However, if you can deal with their complexity and extensive record-keeping requirements (which you likely have the aptitude for considering that you are starting a business in a field that is very paperwork-heavy!), corporations have a key advantage: they limit your personal liability as the owner!

Finally, there's the **Limited Liability Company (LLC)**, which is a *hybrid* structure that combines the simplicity and flexibility of a sole proprietorship or partnership with the limited liability of a corporation. This means that as the owner, you are protected from personal liability for the company's debts and obligations, to an extent. So, if the company fails, you *personally* are not held at fault the same way you would be as a sole proprietor.

This is why most businesses, even if they are owned by one person, will still tend to be registered as LLCs.

When making your choice, think about different factors, such as how much control you want to have, how vulnerable you can be to lawsuits, the tax implications and how they might affect you, as well as your potential future needs. Here, you could also ask for a professional's opinion on the matter, such as a lawyer, who will be able to give you more personalized advice that fits your specific needs depending on your exact goals. Likewise, your business structure isn't set in stone! Your business will grow and change, and you might find it beneficial to change the structure, which is possible in the long-run too. However, changing this structure can be complicated as well as potentially costly, so do take the time *now* to make an informed decision so you can save yourself time, money, as well as stress in the future.

Registering for State and Local Taxes

The next step is to register for state and local taxes. Of course, this might not be the most exciting part of starting your own tax business, but it's still very important (as I am sure you know!). Paying taxes is not just your civic duty, but it's also a critical part of operating a *legitimate* and *compliant* business. You will have federal taxes, as well as state and sometimes jurisdictional taxes to pay. This might include sales taxes, property taxes, and unemployment insurance taxes, among others. The type and amount of tax your business must pay often depends on the nature of your business and its location, so do your research on this!

The first step here is to **determine the type of taxes your business will need to pay**. As a service-based business like a tax consultancy, you may or may not need to pay sales tax, depending on your state and local tax. Each state has its own sales tax regulations, so it's essential to do your homework here (especially as a tax business!).

Next up, if you plan to hire employees, you'll need to consider **unemployment insurance tax**. This tax is typically paid to the state where your employees work. The rate can vary based on all kinds of factors, including the number of employees you have, the rate of turnover in your business, and whether your business is new or established. If you are the only employee in your business, as an LLC, you might still have to pay for it to make sure that *you* are covered if your business fails and you are back on the job market soon after.

Then, depending on your location, your business might also be responsible for additional **local taxes.** For example, some cities and counties impose their own sales taxes, property taxes, or gross receipts taxes (many in California, for example). To determine your local tax obligations, check with your city or county's tax office or a local tax professional. This is something you may also need to know yourself, especially if you plan to offer tax services to business owners! So, think of it as a two-birds-one-stone event.

You will then need to make sure that you have registered with the right tax authorities. As Caleb Hammer, a prominent YouTuber who looks at people's finances and helps them out always says, "the IRS wants their money!" So, you will need to submit the right forms, investigate how much you will have to pay and keep track of the deadlines. As you know as a tax expert, you need to keep track of the details to avoid missing tax deadlines which can lead to serious penalties and interest charges.

The tax registration aspect of your business isn't glamorous—I know that from when I started my own business! —but it's *still* essential. So, be aware of your tax obligations, know when payments are due, and lead by example! As a tax consultant, your very own taxes should be executed perfectly.

Opening Your Business Bank Account

Next, you need a business bank account. Even as a sole proprietor (if this is the structure you are choosing for your business), you will need a separate account for your business expenses. This will make things far simpler once it is time to file the taxes for your business. Managing other people's finances might come easily to you, but it may also be something you dislike doing when it is *your* finances that are at play. If this is the case, having a business account is *even more important* because it will simplify this aspect of running a business.

You may be wondering why you cannot simply use your personal account, especially if you are registered as a sole proprietorship. Well, there are many reasons why establishing a separate account for your business is not just a good idea—it's a **necessity**. Firstly, it simplifies your accounting by keeping your personal and business transactions *separate*, which is important for moments when you, for example, go to conferences and have business expenses that you can deduct later. This makes it easier to track your income and expenses and provides a clearer picture of your business's financial health as well, so you know what is working well, what you might need to improve upon, where you might be spending too much, and so on. For example, having a separate account might reveal that you are spending too much on travel and hence, you may need to either increase your prices or change how you conduct meetings and client calls (could they be done on Zoom instead of traveling to meet clients in person?). Your business bank account also adds a layer of legal protection, especially if you have an LLC or a corporation. Here, mixing personal and business finances could undermine that structure and potentially expose you to personal liability for business debts. On the other hand, if all your expenses (business) are paid from your business account, you remain liable for any debts incurred by the business, even if you are the sole owner of the organization. This also makes you appear much more professional. Specifically, payments made to and from a business account reinforce your brand as a business and therefore help to build trust with your clients and suppliers.

Choosing a bank for your business isn't a decision to rush—you want the best terms possible! Just as you took the time to select a suitable business name, your choice of bank deserves careful consideration too so you are certain of your choice. After all, this is a bank account you will most likely keep for the foreseeable future, so you need to make a decision that considers various factors. Different banks offer different perks, fees, and accessibility options, so shop around for a bank that suits your business's specific needs. Some factors to consider might also include whether the bank offers a dedicated business banking team, online and mobile banking, and how their fees align with your projected business activity. Again, if you are not comfortable making decisions about how to set up bank accounts for your business, you shouldn't hesitate to reach out to a professional for help!

Now that you've chosen a bank, you need the right **documentation** to open a business account. This might include, for example, your business' legal name as well as its structure, your Employer Identification Number, and your personal identification. Call the bank in advance to confirm this before you head over for a meeting (if it is necessary, as not all banks will require you to meet with them face-to-face), to make sure that you have all the necessary documents to take this step.

Get Insured

As a business, if something goes wrong, you can be sued and held liable. Insurance is therefore like a sturdy umbrella that shields you from unexpected downpours. It's there to protect your business from unforeseen risks and liabilities, and to make sure that you are safe regardless of what happens. If you make a mistake on your client's tax returns, or if you miscalculate something, this insurance is there to make sure that you don't go bankrupt. For example, you may benefit from **Errors and Omissions (E&O) insurance**. In the tax business, your advice and service *directly* impact your clients' financial wellbeing. If a client were to allege that your service caused them financial loss—for instance, because of an error in a tax return that you filed for them—professional liability insurance would cover the cost of defending your business and any resulting settlements or judgments as well, making sure that you can keep on running your business even if this one specific time, it didn't work out as planned.

You should also consider **general liability insurance**. This is a kind of insurance that will protect your business against claims like bodily injury or property damage. For example, if a client were to trip and fall in your office, general liability insurance would cover medical costs and legal fees. If you won't be meeting with clients in your office, this may not be applicable to you. However, before you say, *"as if someone would sue if they tripped on my floor,"* yes, yes they would. You might not expect it to happen, but that doesn't mean that it won't happen! It's best to be insured against these unforeseen events to make sure that you can continue doing what you do best, which is helping people with their taxes.

You will also want to consider **property insurance**, especially if you will be meeting with clients in your home office to conduct your tax business. Property insurance can cover the cost of repairing or replacing your business equipment, furniture, and even the building itself in case of damage from fires, storms, or theft, which is great to ensure you won't lose your entire business in case something goes wrong.

Finally, you will need to have other kinds of insurance if you hire employees. However, for now, we are focusing primarily on your insurance needs as an entrepreneur. To learn more about the kind of insurance you may need once you are ready to hire employees, make sure to do your research specifically *within your state* as this will be very different from one state to the next.

On that note, this concludes this chapter. Thus far, we have extensively explored the steps involved in starting your own business. Once you have registered all the important information—including your business name, tax number and licenses—you are ready for the next step, which is setting up your services and pricing. Let's have a look!

CHAPTER SIX

SERVICES AND PRICING

As a tax consultant, you are most likely already somewhat aware of the services you will be selling. However, there may be *more* services that you could offer in the future. Once you have a clear idea of exactly what services you will be offering, you can also start thinking about the prices you will charge. This can be a tough part of starting a business. So, throughout this chapter, we will be examining the details and options.

What Services Will You Be Offering?

As discussed in the previous chapters, there are quite a few potential tax services that you can offer. The services you choose to offer will directly impact the kind of audience that you attempt to reach through your marketing efforts (which we will discuss later), but if you are new to the world of taxes, it may also affect the kind of training you undergo to become qualified to help others.

To start with, think about your **skill set as well as your area of expertise**. Are you, for example, an expert in personal income tax, in corporate tax, or perhaps in international tax law? If you already have some knowledge in these areas, your proficiency will shape your service offerings, forming the bedrock upon which your business is built. Remember, it's important to offer services that you are competent and comfortable with, as this assures high-quality service delivery and fosters client trust. For example, I started by providing services to my friends and family members, and I only took on what I felt comfortable with to make sure that I was able to offer clients a valuable and helpful service.

Next, you can also consider it from the opposite point of view: what target market would you like to attract? For this, try to imagine the typical tax problems that your potential clients might be dealing with. Are they small business owners struggling with tax compliance? Or maybe they're individuals seeking help with tax planning and filing? Your aim should be to **provide solutions tailored to these needs**. This is a good way to evaluate what kind of services you might want to provide. Of course, the goal is to determine where your expertise and your audience's needs intersect. For example, you could offer tax preparation and filing, tax planning and advice, tax resolution services, or even bookkeeping and payroll services, all depending on the kind of skills that you have to offer.

As you define your portfolio, aim for *balance*. There should be a balance between the breadth and depth of the services you are offering. The range might help you attract many diverse clients, but you do not want to be spreading yourself too thin. So, make sure that your offerings showcase your specialized skills and deliver high quality services your clients need. In fact, specialization is especially important as a tax consultant or expert. Concentrating on a specific niche helps you distinguish yourself from the competition. This doesn't mean that you are *limiting* yourself—quite the opposite. Instead, it means that you are becoming an expert in a specific area, while also expanding your knowledge and skills. So, you can become the go-to tax person for anyone looking for the specific skills and knowledge you possess combined with the excellent customer service and value-added services that are unique to your business.

As you develop your portfolio, remember that it isn't static! The laws will continue to change, new policies will keep emerging, and your clients' needs will continue to evolve. You need to remain relevant and competitive so always be willing to pivot to gain additional skills or hone existing skills to better meet the changing needs of your clients. Review and update your services based on the changes you are seeing in tax laws, market trends, as well as client feedback, so you continuously remain the top choice for those looking for tax-related services.

Market Pricing: Setting Competitive Rates

As a business owner, your goal is naturally to make money. However, as you may know, this is easier said than done. Thankfully, as a tax business, your overhead costs are rather low, especially if you primarily work online and do not have a physical office (though you may want to remember that some clients will prefer working with you face to face, so an office may be necessary depending on your target audience). With this in mind, you can make quite a significant amount, even if you do not have an extensive list of clients yet. Why? Because tax consultants are in high demand, and people are willing to pay big bucks to make sure that their taxes are filed properly and on time, especially since it normally results in significant positive impacts to their bottom line!

Pricing not only determines your revenue and profitability, but it also communicates your business's value to your potential clients. In other words, if your prices are too low, they may wonder why that's the case. If the prices are too high, however, you may be pricing yourself out of a lot of potential business, which isn't ideal either. So, the goal is to find the perfect "in between," which will require some research. The first step, then, is to consider pricing as a **strategic tool rather than just a monetary amount.** It's not simply about covering your costs and generating a profit, though these are indeed important. Pricing also conveys the **value and quality of your services**, which then influences the positioning of your business in your market. Change your mindset when it comes to your profit—it's about much more than just making money. It encapsulates a strategy too!

Then, start thinking about your market in a strategic manner too. Specifically, conducting a **comprehensive market analysis** is going to be your very first step towards understanding pricing in your specific industry. To know how much to charge, you need to know how much others are charging, and consequently, how much you *might* be able to charge depending on how many potential clients you already have, whether you already have a well-established relationship in your field or are starting from the bottom, and so on. For example, I started out already having some clients and experience, especially after having done my friends' and family members' taxes for them for many years, so I already had a client base. Then, I met the woman who inspired me to start my own tax business, so again, I already knew how much I could potentially charge, especially after working for a tax company. If you do not have this kind of experience, explore how your competitors are pricing their services. Are they using hourly rates, fixed fees, or value-based pricing? Simply mirroring your competitors' pricing is not recommended as it may appear unprofessional to clients if they are familiar with your competition. The information you gain from a comprehensive market analysis can be used to understand the market norms and expectations.

When considering the pricing structure you will adopt, think about your costs, your desired profit margin, and the value you provide to your clients. Think about both your direct and indirect costs—direct costs being software or any other tools used for tax preparation, and indirect costs like utilities, rent, and staff salaries (if you have any staff). Then, think about your profit margin. What do you want to be making? Do you think this is feasible? You can again check online to find a range of prices other tax businesses are charging, or you can ask other tax professionals in your area about their typical take-home.

Remember that with taxes, people are typically ready to pay more if they perceive that they're getting exceptional value for their money. Taxes are complicated and time con-suming, so people are willing to pay the price if they believe that the service they will receive is worth the investment! So, it's incredibly important that you communicate the value and the benefits that your services include, which can then justify charging a higher rate.

Depending on the services you are offering, you might need to adjust your strategy. Specifically, individual services and package deals might also need different strategies. You might, for example, offer a flat fee for a simple tax return, but use value-based pricing for more complex advisory services.

As you start out, you might find that you need to keep your prices low until you have your first few clients. Then, you can start increasing your prices as you go. That being said, be aware that previous clients might not be happy if you've doubled your rates by the time they need your services again the next year. So, you may want to advertise "introductory prices," for example, such as an early-bird price for your very first clients. This way, they will expect to see your prices increase over the next few tax seasons, instead of being hit with unexpected price hikes that are twice or even three times what they budgeted to pay.

Just as for any other business, evaluating the demand for your services is the best way to know whether your rates are attracting clients or whether you might need to change your pricing strategy. If you find that you have too much demand and you cannot handle all of it, it may be time to increase your prices slightly. If, on the other hand, you find yourself struggling to find clients, you may need to lower your prices and to focus on what you can do to make your business offerings more appealing. Perhaps you will need to use some marketing techniques that you haven't tried before (more on this shortly), or you may have to revisit your services to pinpoint whether the problem may be that your services aren't tailored to meet the needs of your target audience. Otherwise, your problem might be transparency (or rather a lack thereof)—your clients will appreciate knowing upfront how much your services will cost. Clear, upfront pricing also helps build trust and avoids any unexpected surprises for your clients down the line (which is also why you need to be clear on your price increases from the get-go).

Offering Package Deals and Discounts

While you might want to start with basic services at first, consider offering more specific packages and deals as you grow your business. The more enticing the package, the more you can expect clients to be interested in working with you. After all, a package that highlights the value that your clients get from your services and makes them feel like they are benefiting from the deal of a lifetime might be the best way to attract their business. A package not only seems like a good *financial* deal—it also offers your clients a great deal in terms of the stress relief they get from the experience. As a tax expert, you might love dealing with taxes and numbers. Yet, the reality is that most people truly dislike the experience! So, when you offer them a package deal that takes care of everything related to their taxes from A to Z, you thereby *also* offer them a deal that lowers their stress. We live busy lives where we constantly have responsibilities to fulfill, so when we cancan delegate some of these to someone else, naturally, we feel a gigantic weight lifted off our shoulders. That means you are assuming the responsibility when you take on the work—and your clients are willing to pay you for this! So, the packages you set up should help them feel like you are taking as much work and stress off their shoulders as possible.

Then, you can also consider discounts or deals (such as the introductory offer mentioned in the previous section). You might be interested in providing a promotional discount to attract your new clients, or a loyalty discount to retain your existing customers. Regardless of what you are trying to achieve, try to carefully strategize your discount policy. If you offer *too many discounts*, you might dilute your brand value and hurt your profitability, to the point that customers may feel like they can always find a way around paying the full price. Otherwise, if you do not offer any discounts, or too few, you may be considered a less attractive option, or your clients may not feel like their business is valued.

You could offer, for example, seasonal discounts during peak tax filing periods or referral discounts for clients who bring in new business. The goal is not only to get new customers, but also to retain the ones you have by giving them something back as a small "thank you." You could also offer discounts to specific groups, such as veterans, seniors, or small business owners who are looking for cheaper alternatives but who are still looking for your help. Your discounts should, however, *not* compromise your profitability. This means that you should be clear about *why* you are offering a discount so your customers and new clients can understand that this is a one-time deal, so they don't expect it to be offered in the future. Make sure that you *always* consider the long-term impact of your discounts on your clients' perception of your brand and services.

Upselling and Cross-Selling

Upselling involves recommending a superior, more expensive product to a customer. In your case, it could mean suggesting a comprehensive tax planning package to a client who initially came to you for a simple tax return service. Upselling is somewhat like a gentle nudge towards a higher-end service that offers more value, benefits, and, consequently, costs more, making you more money.

The art of upselling lies in *truly* understanding your client's needs and subtly highlighting how the premium service can address those needs more comprehensively—but importantly, this needs to be done with the client's best interest at heart, as otherwise, this may appear to be disingenuous, which is counterproductive when trying to offer your clients the best possible service. Timing is crucial here! The upsell should be offered as a **natural part of the conversation** and not as an aggressive sales pitch, since your potential customers will otherwise feel like they are being forced or pressured to do something. You need to build a rapport with your client, gain their trust, and understand their requirements before suggesting a more valuable, and thus expensive, service. This is especially true in our industry! We are dealing with people's finances, something that is already very stress-inducing. So, we don't want to *add* to their stress by pushing them to spend more. Instead, we want to encourage them to do what feels right while also giving them some guidance regarding what a good service for them might be based on what they are looking for.

Another technique is called **cross-selling**. This strategy involves suggesting additional, complementary services to your clients. For instance, if a client approaches you for tax filing services, you might cross-sell by suggesting they might also benefit from retirement tax planning or business tax advice if they own a small business. Think of it like the *"other customers who purchased this also purchased..."* suggestions when you purchase something online. The goal is to sell extras to increase your bottom line, and this is something you can do by adding services to your offering that match what your clients are looking for.

The beauty of cross-selling is that it not only increases your revenue per client but also provides a more comprehensive service to your clients, which of course increases their satisfaction. Just like upselling, successful cross-selling is based on **understanding your clients' needs** and suggesting additional services that can genuinely benefit them, and not just offering extras to make more money. You need to offer services that appeal to both what your clients *want* and need. This might sound simple at first, but it is something you need to really spend some time thinking about before you launch your business to ensure that you do not offer a service that isn't in demand (which is a waste of your resources and time).

Remember that your primary role is to **provide professional tax services and help your clients navigate their tax situation efficiently**. Therefore, ensure that these strategies do not come across as aggressive sales tactics. Rather, sales should be a *natural outcome* of the exemplary services you provide and not the other way around.

Also, it's important to train your team in these strategies (if you do have a team)! They should understand how to identify opportunities for upselling and cross-selling and how to present these options to clients tactfully (without coming off too aggressive, and without coming across as though they are pushing your client to purchase services that they don't need just to make your business more money).

Keep 'Em Coming Back! Client Retention and Repeat Business

If you have ever worked in business, you know that retaining clients is one of, if not *the best way* to keep your business afloat. When business slows down or when the economy suffers and you lose a few clients or struggle to find new ones, your loyal customers will be

there to give you their repeat business. Building a solid base of loyal clients is a great way to ensure sustainable growth and prosperity, so maintaining their loyalty through efforts to keep them coming back, incentives to make them feel valued, and rewarding them for their referrals are all things you need to prepare for! A retained client is not just a source of recurring revenue, but also a potential ambassador for your services. It's someone who can spread the word about your business in their network. In fact, retaining a customer is cheaper than attracting and onboarding a new one (especially in terms of marketing dollars).

So, how can you retain your clients? Throughout my career as a tax expert, I have *always* focused on providing exemplary service. As service providers, we need to remember the following: clients don't just buy your *services*; they buy an **experience**. Every interaction with your client, whether it's a consultation meeting, a phone call, or an email conversation, contributes to shaping this experience. You should do all that you can to make this experience as seamless, professional, and pleasant as possible for your clients.

This also includes **consistent communication!** Your clients want to know that you are on top of things. So, you will need to reach out to them regularly, even if it's outside the tax season. You can also provide them with useful tax tips, inform them about the latest tax changes, wish them happy birthday or send happy holidays cards, etc. The idea is that the more you stay in contact with them, the more you show that you are involved in their financial well-being and that you genuinely care about them as clients (and not just for their business!).

You can also showcase the importance you place on customer loyalty by asking for **feedback**. Ask your clients to provide feedback on your services, and make sure that you address their concerns promptly and professionally. This shows your customers that you are committed to improving your services and to enhancing client satisfaction to make sure that they enjoy working with you and feel fulfilled.

The more you show your customers and clients that you care about their business, the more you will get *repeat* business. To further encourage it, however, consider offering loyalty discounts, provide exceptional customer service, and constantly remind your clients about the benefits of your services (without sounding too pushy or self-absorbed!).

Ultimately, the more you impress your clients and give them the kind of service they are looking for, the more you will incentivize them to keep coming back to you. Finances are a tough part of life to take care of, and as a tax expert, you can either help improve your clients' financial well-being while making them feel valued and supported or offer them poor service and a bad experience which will encourage them to look for another tax professional. As you can imagine, the better the experience, the more likely they are to come back to you.

That brings us to the end of this chapter. Now that you know how to *keep* clients, you also need to learn how to *find* clients. Thus, the next chapter will cover how to market and advertise your tax business using various tools and skills.

CHAPTER SEVEN

MARKETING AND ADVERTISING YOUR TAX BUSINESS

With the tips outlined in the previous section, you are all set to keep your new clients coming back. However, for these clients to indeed keep coming back, you first need to attract them to your business which starts with potential clients being able to find you! Throughout this chapter, we will be exploring how you can market and advertise your business to find your first few clients. In business, there are two primary ways to find clients: you can find them through advertising your business (where they hear *about you*), or you can reach out to them through direct marketing (where they hear about you *from* you). The technique you choose depends on what you prefer, how large your audience is, and more. Let's have a look.

What's Different About You?

Ask any business owner for their Unique Selling Proposition (USP), and they should be able to respond relatively quickly and clearly. Your USP is what sets you apart from the competition. It's a specific benefit or feature that makes your business *unique*. It could be something about your services, your process, your team, or even your own personal approach that's distinctive and valuable (such as your experience, how you approach tax returns, etc.). It's not just about being different, but about offering something that matters to your clients and is not readily available elsewhere! For example, let's say that you have worked as a tax professional for another small business for over a decade. This is a great start *and* something that gives you a lot of credibility, but it isn't "unique" per se. On the other hand, if throughout these years you came up with a process that has helped many clients save over $5,000 per year, then you *are* different. Think about how you are different, what makes you different, and what makes you a better choice than the competition. This is what your audience wants to know, and they need to have access to that information quickly!

To find your USP, start by looking inwardly. What kind of strengths do you bring to the business, and what special skills or experiences do you bring as well? What are you particularly good at? What parts of your work do you love the most? What kind of value do you bring to your clients that no one else tends to bring? Then, compare this to others (the one time when comparing yourself to others can be handy!): what are they doing well? What are they doing less-well, and where are they falling short? Pinpointing this will help you identify gaps in the market that you can then fill.

Of course, you need to think about your clients before anything else. What are their pain points? What do they value most when it comes to tax services? You can survey existing and potential clients to find out more or have in-depth conversations with your clients to learn more. The idea is to use your strengths to meet the needs that you identify in your market. This is how you find a USP that is compelling *and* relevant!

Target Audience and Segmentation: Who Are You Targeting?

Before you start any kind of marketing efforts, you need to know who you are trying to reach with your campaign. By now, you should have a general idea of who you are targeting roughly speaking, such as people looking for international tax services, individuals, small businesses, and the like (if not, don't worry—you can continue to refine your market after reading this book). When you know your target market, you can segment it into smaller audiences that you can then target accordingly.

So, start by considering your **target audience**. This is the specific group of people who are most likely to require your tax services. This can be as broad as all the business owners in the city (though this makes it difficult to specialize), or as specific and narrow as independent contractors in the tech industry who work remotely. The goal is to find a balance so your target audience is specific *enough* to be distinct, but also broad enough to sustain your business.

Think about the **demography** as well. How old are they? How much money are they making? Where do they live? What occupation do they have? Then, don't stop there! Go *beyond* the numbers and look at psychographics: their attitudes, behaviors, and pain points. What are their financial goals? What tax issues keep them up at night? Do they prefer a conservative or an aggressive approach to tax planning? The more you know about what they are looking for, the better you can cater to these needs and wishes. Similarly, the more you know about your audience, the easier the next step is—segmentation.

Segmentation involves dividing your target audience into smaller and more specific groups based on the characteristics they share. For example, they might be in the same industry, make be of the same business size, or may have specific tax issues. For example, within the broader group of "small business owners," you might have segments such as "restaurant owners," "retail store owners," and "freelance designers." This segmentation is necessary for you to create tailored marketing messages that speak directly to the needs and desires of each segment. Likewise, the more you know about your market, the more you know about the services they are looking for! For example, the restaurant owners might be mainly struggling with sales tax, while freelance designers might be more concerned with managing their irregular income. The more information you have on your various segments, the more you can target and personalize the services you are offering!

SEO, Social

Media

and

Email Marketing

When targeting new clients, you need to think of how you can reach them. One way to do this is through marketing. And while there are traditional ways to advertise your services, currently, online marketing tends to be a better option (although if you want to work primarily with people who do not tend to be online, you may *not* want to go online and may want to stick to traditional methods instead.

Assuming that you are interested in primarily using online marketing methods, also called *digital marketing,* you will want to start by learning more about **SEO**. Please note that in today's connected world, digital marketing is no longer *optional*; it's a tool that you **must** have in your arsenal to attract, engage, and retain clients. Not having an online presence is a surefire way to present yourself as a company that isn't very reliable. So, you need SEO! SEO refers to Search Engine Optimization, and it is the process of increasing the visibility of your website or online content in search engine results pages. Simply explained, it is about making it easier for your potential clients to find you when they're searching for tax services online. For a website to be "SEO compatible," you need to leverage various aspects of your website, such as its content, the design and the keywords you use throughout the content, and hyperlinks. The goal isn't only to get more traffic (visitors), but to get the right kind of traffic (i.e., "leads" that are likely to *lead* to converted clients). So, your SEO needs to be in line with what you are offering and must bring in people who are searching for services like the ones you are offering.

Businesses need to be using **social media** to engage potential clients and retain current clients. Nowadays, you have many options to choose from! Platforms like Facebook, Twitter, LinkedIn, and Instagram offer a unique opportunity to connect with your clients on a *personal level*—more personal than ever before! You can use social media to share tips, to update your customers, or to be more available so potential clients can inquire on the kinds of services you offer. Your social media accounts are also a way for your clients to leave a review or to engage with your content so you get more visibility online. To make the most out of social media, make sure that you are posting consistently, that you are engaging with your audience, and that you are sharing content that is valuable *and* relevant to your clients.

Email Marketing is another technique you can use. In fact, email is still one of the most effective digital marketing channels, even despite social media! It's a direct line of communication between you and your clients, so it is ideal for you to send personalized messages and offers as needed. This means that you can send personalized messages and offers, newsletters, or simply updates. The fact that email is likely to be your main channel of communication for tax-related issues also means that your clients are likely to open your marketing emails too! You can use email marketing to send reminders, such as right before tax season starts, to make sure that they remember that they need to contact you to schedule an appointment and then send you their information to get their taxes done on time.

Besides digital options, you also have traditional advertising methods, as briefly mentioned earlier. Don't forget about the tried-and-true techniques such as going to events, joining professional organizations, or leveraging your personal contacts. Online or digital marketing is very useful to attract a completely new clientèle, but this doesn't mean that you can't use good old-fashioned ones as well! Make sure that you have brochures, business cards, and that you are using print ads and direct mail where needed. You could also raise awareness of your services by hosting tax workshops, participating in local events or being involved in your community so you become known as the go-to person for tax-related issues.

Creating a Marketing Plan

The same way we created a business plan to help give you a detailed road map for launching your business, a marketing plan can greatly help guide and target your advertising efforts. This plan will help you figure out what your goals are, how to develop a marketing strategy, and the resources you will need to implement your plan. So, first, start by aligning your marketing plan with your overall business goals. Do you want to attract a certain number of new clients this year? Expand into a new market segment? Increase client retention rates? To make them happen, establish **clear, specific, and measurable goals** that will guide your marketing efforts.

Then, you can start working on your strategies, using the information you have on your target audience and your unique selling proposition (as discussed in the previous sections). Your marketing plan should include a **mix of digital and traditional marketing methods** to cater to each target audience segment, and to maximize your chances of being seen, contacted and hired. Each strategy should be chosen and designed with your audience in mind. For SEO, which keywords will you target? For social media, which platforms will you use, and what type of content will you share? For networking, where and how will you forge new connections?

Next, make sure that your **strategies are all specific** in terms of the goals you want to achieve. For example, what do you want your conversion percentage to be whenever you send a marketing email? Similarly, think about the kind of **budget** you have. How much do you have? What will you do to make sure you stay on track?

Then, finally, make sure that you have a plan to track and evaluate how well your marketing strategies are doing. Which metrics will you use to measure your success? How often are you going to review your progress and adjust your strategies? Consider whether it's easier to work with an advertising company, especially if you are new to marketing and don't know what will work best? If this isn't your forte, it's okay to ask for help!

Your marketing plan then becomes the foundation of your marketing strategy. Of course, I could go on and on about this topic, but the details are best left to a marketing expert to cover, not a tax expert like me! Next is the final chapter of the book where I will be providing you with my best tips and tricks on how to grow and potentially expand your business in the long term.

CHAPTER EIGHT

GROWING AND EXPANDING YOUR BUSINESS

If you are primarily focused on starting a small business, this is absolutely possible. However, if your goal is to eventually create a business in which you lead other tax consultants and advisors where your main tasks will be primarily to manage the process, you obviously want to *expand* and *grow* your business further. If you are a lone wolf, this may not be the ideal plan for you. However, if the idea of managing a big tax consultancy organization sounds like a dream to you, then this chapter is for you!

Performance Analysis and KPI Tracking

Whenever you are trying to grow something, namely a business, you need to be tracking your performance. This is something you can only do by analyzing and tracking Key Performance Indicators (KPIs). For example, will you be tracking the number of new customers you get each month? Or looking at how much profit you are making each quarter. Then, you need to ask yourself how you will implement monitoring and tracking systems for this—will you be doing this yourself? Will you download software that does it for you? Will you hire a third-party company to help you with this aspect of your company? These companies can help you implement systems that allow you to monitor and track data. Similarly, they allow you to interpret and utilize your data for business growth while providing you with regular performance reviews. So, these software and/or tracking systems can be worth the investment if you aim to grow your business significantly.

Expansion Strategies

When expanding your business, you have various strategies that you can try. For example, you can start by identifying potential new markets (i.e., new demographics, new geographic areas, psychographic considerations, etc.), and you can also develop new services based on your clients' needs and market demand. You could also primarily focus on product diversification, mainly by adding complementary services to bring in the clients who were getting these services elsewhere before. The goal is always to look for what clients and potential customers are looking for and to give them exactly what they want and need.

Preparing for the Future

The future is uncertain, that's all that we can be certain of! The more you grow your business, the more likely you may be to gain the attention of people who are potentially interested in buying your company from you. You may, for example, be presented with the opportunity to merge your company with someone else's, or your company may be acquired by another one if you choose to accept their offer. You may have different kinds of opportunities, especially as your business grows steadily. Remember that you are doing this to help people with their taxes—and keep their financial well-being at heart at all times!

Selling Your Business

After working hard to build a business, you may be tempted to sell it if the opportunity presents itself. If this is the case, make sure that you have a solid strategy in place! You will want to prepare your business for sale by increasing its value and attractiveness, and you will want to find potential buyers to then negotiate the sale. You may also want to get legal and financial support throughout the process to make sure that you are making sound decisions before you sign any kind of contract.

Although short, hopefully this chapter provided you with some insights into what to expect in the future when it comes to your business. Starting a new business is a great opportunity for future growth, and the sky is the limit! On that note, head over to the conclusion for a few final words on the matter.

Chapter Nine

Conclusion

Your tax business, which perhaps was just an idea at the start of this book, is a dream that *can* come true. If I was able to do a complete 180 and start my own business after working in sales in a car dealership, you can switch up your career and start your own tax business too! All you need is the information to get started, the will to work hard, and the dedication and discipline to keep going even when things keep testing you and your resilience.

Becoming a tax expert is not something that *everyone* can do, but after reading this book in its entirety, it absolutely is something that *you* are equipped to do. Now's the time to get started!

On a final note, thank you sincerely for taking the time to read this book! I am always here if you have any questions, and I wish you all the best with your endeavors.

Sincerely,

Nathaniel McDaniel

About the Author

Nathaniel R. McDaniel studied accounting and business at Eastern Oklahoma State College. He has owned Refund Man Taxes in Arlington, TX since 2008 which has been ranked the #1 tax service in the Dallas/Fort Worth area.

Married with four children and three grandchildren, McDaniels enjoys spending time with his 4-year-old daughter—taking her to her karate and gymnastics lessons. An avid traveler, he has been on 18 cruises and travels to Dallas Cowboys, Pittsburgh Steelers, and Oklahoma Sooner College football games with his eldest son and brother.